How to Raise
Backyard Chickens

The Complete Guide to Caring for
Chicks to Laying Hens

Introduction

Before we get started, I would like to thank you and congratulate you for purchasing this book, *"How to Raise Backyard Chickens: The Complete Guide to Caring for Chicks to Laying Hens"*

Backyard chickens can be a great source of fresh eggs and fun, or even meat (But that's for another book). In this book we will be discussing raising hens for their healthy eggs. Just like any other animals, hens are nice pets to have around. They are low maintenance and offer us a wide range of benefits that other pets don't. You won't need to play with them, groom them or take them for walks. Though you and your chickens may enjoy that time, it is not a requirement like dogs or other such animals. As long as you give them food, water and a nice clean home, your family will enjoy their constant supply of fresh eggs for years to come.

Urban chickens are increasingly becoming popular with home owners due to many of these benefits. In addition, they don't need much space. A proper housing for them, known as a coop can be built easily from home or bought. A chicken coop will need to be strong and effective to ensure your hens are comfortable, healthy and also protect them from predators. It doesn't need to be highly specialized; in fact most people prefer to build it themselves rather than buying one pre made or a kit. This is not only cheaper but allows you to build it to your liking. We shall be getting into more details on chicken coops in a later chapter.

Having backyard chicken means that you won't have to throw away left over food items. Chickens have a big appetite and eat almost anything. They will also be good for your home since they will eat all the ants, worms, small insects that they can find that could otherwise find their way into your home or garden. Even though chickens will feed on almost anything they come around, you need to supplement their food with commercial feeds that will have the right amount of elements they need. For instance, egg-laying hens will need to get adequate amounts of calcium. Broilers and roosters will need their special type of feeds too.

However, don't limit their natural instinct to foraging and range around as they look for snacks, anything from fresh grass to worms will be food for them. Kitchen scraps will be especially good for them. You also need to ensure they have clean water at all times. We will also be looking more into feeding in a later chapter.

All this information and much more will be covered in this book. By the end of your reading, you will be equipped with more than enough knowledge to get started raising your very own backyard chickens. It's fun, exciting, and healthy.

CC0 Public Domain pixabay.com

Contents

Disclaimer

The information herein is geared towards giving definite and dependable data concerning the theme and issue covered. The distribution is sold with the understanding that the distributor, writer or publisher is not qualified or otherwise to give medical, legal or financial advice. In the event that guidance is needed, a legitimate or proficient person in the profession ought to be sought.

The information herein is understood to be truthful. In that any risk, regarding use or misuse, of any approaches, techniques, or direction contained inside is the lone and utter responsibility of the reader. By no means will any legitimate or illegitimate obligation or fault be held against the distributor, publisher, author or other, for any reparation, harms, or money related misfortune because of the data herein, either straightforward or by implication.

The data thus is offered for information purposes only. The presentation of the data is without contract or any kind of insurance certification.

The trademarks that are utilized are without any consent or support by the trademark owner. All trademarks and brands inside this book are for clarifying purposes only and are owned by the owners themselves, not affiliated with this document.

CopyScape Verified May 25, 2015

Edited December 10, 2015

Glossary of Chicken Terms

BANTAM: A small domestic chicken that is often a miniature version of a larger breed.

BROILER: A meat chicken processed at the age of 7-12 weeks when it reaches 2 ½ to 3 ½ pounds live weight. Historically Broilers were marketed as birds ranging 1 to 2 ½ lbs.

BROODER: A temperature-controlled, heated box used for raising newly hatched poultry.

BROODY HEN: A hen that is intent on sitting on and hatching a clutch of eggs on a nest. Broody hens are often used to hatch eggs of other fowl.

CHICK: A newly hatched or very young chicken.

COCK: A male chicken over one year of age.

COCKEREL: A male chicken less than 1 year old.

COMB: The fleshy growth or crest on the top of a chicken's head. Combs are usually larger on males than on females and are typically red.

COOP: An enclosure or housing structure built for chickens.

DEBEAKER: remove the upper part of the beak to prevent it from injuring other birds

DUSTING OR DUST BATH: Common chicken behavior of bathing with dust in a shallow depression to help rid themselves of mites and parasites.

FEEDER: A device or container that provides food.

GIZZARD: Internal chicken organ that crushes food with the help of pebbles or grit.

GRIT: Bits of rock, oyster shell or sand used by fowl to aid in breaking down ingested food.

HEN: A mature female chicken that is at least one year of age.

LAYERS: Mature female chickens kept for egg production. Also known as laying hens.

LAYING FEED: Commercially available feed formulated with extra calcium for laying hens.

LITTER: The bedding material spread on the floor of a chicken house (i.e. wood shavings, straw).

MAREK'S DISEASE: A viral disease common in chickens. Commonly prevented by a vaccination administered immediately after chicks hatch.

MOLT: Time when the shedding and growth of new feathers takes place.

NEST BOX: A box designed for hens to lay their eggs within.

NEWCASTLE DISEASE: A viral respiratory disease common in chickens. Newcastle disease can spread very quickly within a flock. Commonly prevented with a series of vaccinations.

ORNAMENTAL BREED: A breed of chicken used for ornamental purposes and are primarily appreciated for their stunning appearance as opposed to egg or meat production.

PEA COMB: Medium-size comb that features three ridges running lengthwise from the top of the beak to the top of the head and resembles an opened pea pod with peas running up the middle.

PULLET: A chicken less than 1 year old.

ROOSTER: A male chicken that is at least 1 year old.

ROOST: A perch typically inside a coop upon which fowl rest off of the ground.

RUN: An enclosed area outdoors that is connected to a coop and allows chickens to roam freely.

SCRATCH: A type of feed that can consist of cracked corn and different types of whole grains. It is often fed as a treat for backyard chickens and not used as a main food source.

SEXING: When baby chicks are separated by gender.

STARTER FEED: Pre-mixed commercial food for chicks, commonly available at feed or farm stores. These feeds should be fed to chicks for the first six to eight weeks of life. Typically available in medicated and non-medicated formulas.

WATERER: A device or container that provides water

Chapter 1: Space Required and Coop Size

Hens will require both a coop and an outside space which is called a "chicken run". The coop is the fixed structure where they spend the night, lay eggs or can go into to take cover from harsh weather. The run is where they'll spend their day. Chickens by their very nature are very active, rarely will you find a hen just lazing around. They are always scratching, moving, or taking a sand bath. Thus they need an area where they can do this. It is recommended that you choose to cover the run with some mesh/fencing type of material but you should make sure to allow sunlight to get through. This will make sure your hens happy and healthy.

Chickens will require a minimum of 4 square feet of coop space per hen. They'll also require a minimum of 10 square feet of run area. These are the recommended sizes which will determine the number of hens you'll be able to have, depending on the space you have around your home. You can decide to do away with the run area and only house the chickens in a coop. This will not be ideal for them. If space is limited though, this is a possible option. In this case, you'll need 10 square feet of coop space per every hen. In some locations, this will be the only viable alternative. If you live in an area that experiences winter for several months of the year, then the run area might not be practical because during the winter month, your chickens will need to be housed inside the coop. The run area will mostly be used in the warmer months of the year.

The run area doesn't need to have any particular shape. A rectangle, square and even circular would do. The trick here would be finding the best area for your chickens so that they are not in the way of any of your other daily activities. If you have a small garden where you plant vegetables, you will need to keep it apart from the run area unless you plan for it to be a chicken buffet. A side yard would make a good run area. Those long spaces beside a house and the fence would be ideal. Any other area you choose will still do, provided you meet the minimum of 10 square feet per bird. The run area should be grass or dirt. If you do not have these options you should cover the asphalt or cement with some type of material such as straw, leaves, sawdust or woodchips. This will ensure that the chickens have something to scratch on and some insects to feed on, but most importantly it will act as an absorbent for the smell of the chickens manure and make it easier to clean. Remember these animals are near your house or a neighbor's house and I am sure you don't want these smells lingering around. The mulch helps the manure decompose naturally without the smell. Chicken poop is also fairly toxic and can make the soil fairly acidic. The mulch will help to counter this, especially because most people will regularly change the run areas to plant vegetables on the already fertile space. Hope you are noting all these benefits of backyard chickens! This mulch will need to be added regularly and after a while need to be removed completely. This will be manure which can be used in your garden to support your plants.

CC0 Public Domain pixabay.com

A good run should be properly sealed off with strong materials all along. The advantage with this is that since the coop will be inside the run, you won't have to close it. The hens will come out of the coop in the morning and return in the evening without any human help needed. This will serve you well in case you travel or come home late. However, if you live in an area where predators are always lurking, you should be closing off the coop securely in the evening and opening it in the morning. To ensure you do not forget there are many different automatic door options.

CC0 Public Domain pixabay.com

The coop

The main purpose of a chicken coop is to protect the hens from harsh weather, keep them away from predators, and a place to nest and lay eggs. You can choose to buy or build a coop. Buying is relatively more expensive than building one. If you already have some wood, metal, milk crates or plastic scraps around your home, then building your coop will be easy and cheap. You could also build one from bricks or wood pallets. If you have any construction going on in your neighborhood, you could try asking if they have any wood scraps or damaged materials and build your coop from them. If you can't build it yourself, you could hire someone to build it for you.

There are a few considerations to make when deciding on the best coop, whether buying or building. These are mostly dependent on the chicken's needs, your own preferences and the area you live in. Hens are a hardy animal and will survive in a wide range of conditions, some breeds do better in certain climates then others.

They will only need a few things to stay happy and healthy. Let's take a quick look at them.

Lighting

Chickens need light to function normally. Most of their bodily functions are guided by light. That's why you hear roosters crow in the morning even before dawn. They know when it's time to sleep and when to wake up based on the light. It important to make sure that your coop provides enough light for them. Your coop should also allow sun to get through especially if you don't have a run area. You should position your coop in such a way that morning sun will get in through to your chickens. You'll notice how they love it. The spacing for lighting will also enable air circulation which is vital for hens. Most poultry diseases come up due to poor ventilation.

If you live in an area where winter falls hard, you will need to install some form of electrical lighting and heating system for your chickens. This will enable them to survive and still function normally.

CC0 Public Domain pixabay.com

Size

The size of the coop will be dictated by the number of hens you want to keep. Keep in mind the recommended coop size per hen. If you fail to observe the coop size guidelines, your chickens might easily catch diseases, exhibit aggression and cannibalistic tendencies and even break their own eggs.

Budget

This is the other factor in choosing a chicken coop. Your budget is very critical. If you want a low cost, low maintenance coop which will serve you well, then you have that options. If you don't have time to build and don't mind buying one, or if you need to follow by-law or building code regulations, you have that option as well. Your budget will be a key factor in choosing your chicken coop. Determine how much you want to spend on your entire project right from the start. Not only the coop but also all other costs you are likely to incur, such as buying the chicks, buying the feed, paying any city regulatory fees, and electrical costs. Once you have this figure then you will be able to make a better decision regarding the design, and cost of your coop.

Time

Though building a basic coop can be done in a weekend or over a few weekends, not everyone has the time. If this is your case, the only option is to buy one that is premade or to hire someone to build it for you. If you decide to build it yourself I would recommend doing a bit of research into some basic building guides. If you are lacking in time, make sure the design you build or buy is fairly easy to clean.

Location and climate

The other thing to consider is climate. This is very important since the coop must be deigned to protect your chickens all year long. Does your area receive a lot of rain? How long does the winter last? Is it overly windy? These questions will help you determine what kind of coop to have. If it's fairly cold in most months of the year, you should have insulation and temperature control such as heat lamps set up in the coop. if it rains a lot, then you might need to raise your coop above the ground and also have an adequate roof on it to protect your chickens.

Determine a good location to keep your chickens safe from predators. Different areas have different pests. Since chickens don't really have the ability to defend themselves, they have a wide range of predators that may want to enjoy them as a meal. Dogs, cats, raccoons, foxes, wolves, hawks and coyotes are just a few examples. When you identify the type of predators present in your area, build or buy a coop that will withstand their threat. Some of them like dogs can be strong and attempt to destroy the fence; you need strong durable materials. Others will try to find little spaces anywhere in the coop or even try to dig under it. This will require you ensure that your coop is predator proof. You might need to cover the run from the top too. Check around your coop daily and check for signs of animals digging in or the chickens trying to dig out. If you notice digging around your coop you will need to take steps to protect your chickens. One method is digging a 12-24 inch trench and fastening chicken wire to the bottom of your coop then filling in the trench will help prevent a predator from getting in.

CC0 Public Domain pixabay.com

What you need to have in your coop

There are a few things you need to have in your coop to successfully keep your chicken safe and healthy. If you choose to buy a premade coop, you'll have most of these ready-made, but if you built it yourself you have to ensure you provide them.

Roosting poles: hens love sleeping high up on a pole. In fact never let them sleep on the ground as this goes against their instinct. Provide a roosting pole 2 inches wide. A rounded pole would be better since the hens will perch and curl their legs round the pole.

Nesting boxes: nest boxes are where the hens will lay their eggs. They should be raised from the floor but easily accessible. They should be dark and comfortable. Hens like their privacy while laying. Straw, leaves or woodchips will provide a good surface. The nesting box should be out of the way, so that other hens do not disturb the laying hen. You can make your work easier by providing a small door on the outside where you can collect the eggs rather than having to go inside.

Feeders and waterers: you should provide an area to accommodate these. We shall get into a bit more detail on feeders further in this book.

Storage boxes: you'll need some strong storage boxes or containers to keep the chicken feed. The feed can be dusty so you should keep it outside of your house but then again, it can attract rodents. You might wonder why you're going through so much food just to realize you fed all the neighborhood rats. Rodents are a nuisance to chicken farmers since they'll even feed from the chicken feeders and if your area has many of these, you should wire proof your coop so that they don't gain entry. Place a small sized wire mesh or cloth mesh 12 inches deep all around your coop. this will prevent them from burrowing in.

Chapter 2: Choosing a Chicken Breed

You will need to decide on what type of chickens you would like to own. There are over 400 varieties to choose from. For a beginner, it may seem a daunting task. However, choosing the right chicken for your needs is essential as different breeds have different characteristics as well as different uses. Some hens are better egg layers; others are good pets while others are good meat producers. There are also some that are considered dual purpose. You will need to have a good breed to match whatever your needs are for your backyard chickens. If you plan to have chickens, you should get more than two if you have the room and your city by-laws allow. They are very social animals and are always happy in groups. If you want to keep them for eggs; a good guideline would be two hens per family member for a constant supply all year round.

CC0 Public Domain pixabay.com

There are different types of hens, the large fowls, standard size and the bantam. There are some breeds where there are only the bantam sizes available. There is also another distinction of hard and soft feather breeds. You'll have to make a choice between these different varieties. Another consideration when choosing the best chicken will be color of both their feathers and their eggs. Pure breeds will normally have a single color run through their body while hybrid breeds will have several colors. Let's look at some common backyard chicken breeds:

Bantams are mainly kept for ornamental purposes. They weigh 1-2 pounds. They are good pets and good with children. They still lay eggs, which are smaller in size and not as frequently as the other normal sized hens. Breeds such as Sebrights, Silkies and Belgian Bearded D'Uccles are only found as bantams. You could raise bantams and other chicken together. They will not necessarily be bullied due to their size as some can really be dominant.

If you live in a cold area, there are some breeds that will be better for you. These have evolved to withstand lower temperatures. They are fluffy, feather footed and fat to keep warm. Some of these breeds are Plymouth Rocks, Wyandottes, Chanteclers, Orpingtons, Langshans and Sussexes.

CC0 Public Domain pixabay.com

Other breeds thrive in warmer areas. They include White Leghorns, Golden Campines, Blue Andalusians and Light Brown Leghorns. These hens have larger combs and close feathering to keep heat out of their bodies. Turkens are also a good breed. They are the naked neck breed which is fun to have in a flock.

Another consideration to make when choosing a breed would be their capacity to produce eggs. I'll suggest a few breeds which are good layers and also pack some meat. White Leghorns, Stars, Rhode Island Reds, Marans, Plymouth Rocks and Orpingtons.

Another consideration would be egg color. Eggs come in a wide range of colors, Brown eggs, and white eggs, blue, green, cream and different variations of these colors. However, the nutritional composition of an egg can't be determined by the color of the shell. This is a common misconception. The color will depend on the breed and to a smaller extent, the food. If you want to have different colors of eggs, then look for the specific breed among these.

- For blue eggs: Araucanas

- For green/blue eggs: Easter Eggers

- For deep reddish-brown eggs: Barnvelders, Welsummers

- For very dark, chocolate brown eggs: Marans

- For pinkish brown eggs: Plymouth Rocks, Salmon Faverolles

- For cream-colored eggs: Polish, Sussexes

- For white eggs: White Leghorns, Anconas, campines

- For normal brown eggs: Rhode Island Reds, Australorps, New Hampshire Reds, Delawares, Plymouth Rocks,Wyandottes

Where can you buy Hens?

There are various places to buy hens from. I will list some of these here

- A known breeder

If you want to get a pure breed of a certain variety, then a known breeder would be best. Breeders often spend a lot of time improving on their breeds to the point of getting a pure breed. They may be more expensive to buy chicks from but at least you can be sure of what you pay for. They will provide you with all the necessary information about the breed and you can always go back at a later date to seek advice.

- A poultry show

Poultry shows are a good place to buy a chicken from. There will be some sales pens for the exhibiting breeders. This is one purpose of the shows, to connect breeders and farmers and to share information regarding the breeds. All hens that are brought to the show are of good heath as the reputation of the breeder is at line.

- Private hatchers

If you have no preference for any breed and just want a hen, then a private hatcher will be fine. However you don't want to just go with a sickly bird, so you should seek a lot of information and a little feedback if you can.

- Hatch your own

You can decide to hatch your own chicks. Nowadays hatching is pretty easy due to easy availability of incubators. Though this will only be viable for larger scale farmers.

You can buy chickens at various stages in their growth, either as fertilized eggs, day old chicks, older chicks, teenage hens or fully grown hens. If you just want a few backyard eggs for daily supply of fresh eggs, then hatching them won't be a very good idea.

Buying day old chicks and raising them is fairly common practice, it's fun and you really get to learn a lot about the hen from an early age. If you have kids, they'll find it fun as well. However, you must have some time to spare as they'll require considerable attention. You also need to wait for around 5 month before you get your first supply of eggs.

Buying teenage chicken is another option for a home garden. They will be slightly more expensive but will actually have saved you money in the long run since even with the chicks, you will have to buy feeds, buy heat lamps, and look after them more carefully. At this stage, you'll also be sure of the sex of the chicken. It's likely to mix up the hens and the roosters in day old chicks even in expert hatcheries. Imagine the disappointment of raising a chick only to realize several weeks later that it's a cock.

You can also choose to buy a fully grown hen at her prime of egg laying. This will be more expensive but you'll start enjoying the supply of eggs immediately. You however run the risk of buying a hen that has health problems that the owner didn't disclose or an aged chicken that will only lay a few eggs for you per week. Note the egg laying capabilities reduce with age.

Video References

The following videos will show you the growth of chickens in the first 2 months.

Day Old

https://youtu.be/fYVKvxuwF-w

One Week

https://youtu.be/rcikIqlGj-8

Two Weeks

https://youtu.be/UCKX-a3wT_w

Three Weeks

https://youtu.be/vboDlsJwLl8

One Month

https://youtu.be/UfIDDwQPaoM

Five Weeks

https://youtu.be/acnEEHUwHbA

Six Weeks

https://youtu.be/MmtmsJmn8ns

Seven Weeks

https://youtu.be/tZciJS8tzjo

Two Months

https://youtu.be/MscOT5duSWU

Chapter 3: How to Care for Chicks

Young chicks are very delicate to handle. They require lots of care and constant attention. So if you choose to raise hens from day old chicks, you need to make sure that you have no time-consuming engagements or some family member is there for them

CC0 Public Domain pixabay.com

The first thing is assembling all the supplies you need for these chicks well in advance before you bring them forth, You'll require a brooder, heat lamp, feeder and waterer. You also need to designate an area where they'll first stay before they can move in to the coop. Generally chicks require just a little space since they are already small and will be moving to the coop in about four weeks. A garage, workshop, or a specially made coop will do fine. You just need to make sure that the chosen area is predator proof, weather proof and easily accessible at all times. The chosen area should also be safe from scary noises that might make the chicks frightened. They can easily die of fright. If you choose a room with a cement floor, find some cardboard and enclose them to limit their movements. Take note not to create corners as they tend to hurdle around corners and smother each other to death. A cardboard box with some high walls might be sufficient if you just have a few chicks. You will have to cover the floor with some form of bedding. Wood shavings, sawdust, dried up leaves will be good choices. However, since the chicks will have very small and weak legs, you can cover these with a paper towel for the first week. Their legs can easily go different directions in an even surface and break. If this happens there's no cure. If you already had an area where you had previous chicks, it will be important to disinfect to kill any lingering germs. Chicks have weak immune systems that can get easily compromised.

Chicks will need a constant supply of heat that they would normally get from their mother. You need a heat lamp to provide this heat. Test your heat lamp before you bring in the chicks. You should have two for security. if you just have one and it malfunction, your chicks might not survive. A 250 watts infrared heat lamp is recommended since it's not very bright and will provide the required heat. During the first week, they'll need 95 degrees which you will reduce by 5 degrees for each subsequent week. The heat lamp should be suspended right to the area where the chicks will be staying. The suspension mechanism should lower or rise if you need to control the heat. If the chicks are scrambling together, it means they are feeling cold and you need to lower the heat lamp to increase the temperature. If they are going further from the heat source and look restless, raise the heat lamp higher to reduce the temperatures. An adverse temperatures can kill them within hours. That is why we talked about constant attention.

CC0 Public Domain pixabay.com

The paper towels that will serve as bedding will only be good for the first week. Small chicks poop big, since they are constantly feeding. The towels won't keep up with this. By the second week the legs will be strong enough to withstand most types of bedding. You need to make sure that you keep on changing the bedding to make them comfortable and keep them dry.

The chicks will be feeding right from the first day they get to your home. They have enough stock to last them three days from the yolk but they nibble on anything they find even during this time. Provide water and food right from the word go. It's helpful to treat their water with some nutrients to strengthen them. A tablespoon of molasses to 4 liters of water will be good for them. A table spoon of vinegar/apple cider vinegar added to the water will also be good for their immune system. However, if you notice any blood in their poop, you'll need to use a tablespoon of vinegar for every liter of water. The water container should be something small and shallow. You don't have to purchase one; you could easily convert a plate for this purpose. Make sure to change the water every so often. Same for feed, find some container which will be easily accessible to them. You have to start them on commercial feeds right away. Choose the starter feeds which will make them start their development with the needed nutrients.

Small chicks will often be affected by what's normally known as pasty butt. This is the blocking of their vent opening by their caked up droppings. You will need to keep an eye out for this right from taking them out of the box they came in. If not cleared up, this condition will kill them. When you notice it, use a wet cloth or paper towel to gently unblock them. You could also use the paper towel and a tooth pick. If it's really blocked, you have no choice but to dip the chicks' backside into warm water for a short time. Coccidiosis is another common condition which will be present if the chicks are unvaccinated. Medicated feeds from the start will prevent it and if it does occur, a tablespoon of vinegar for every liter of water will save the non-infected chicks.

Chapter 4: When to take them to the Coop

When the chicks are about 4 weeks old, they are ready to move to their permanent home. That is the outside coop. if you were hosting them in a specialized coop, you need to take them where they'll spend their lives. You'll notice that at this age, they have fully grown feathers and will be able to keep warm. This is the same age where the mother hen would start leaving them for periods of time.

CC0 Public Domain pixabay.com

However, before they move, you need to harden them a little so that they don't just suffer a shock from the change. You could start by moving them outside for a few hours during the day, withholding their heat lamp for a few hours and observing how they react. Remember you have been acclimatizing them by reducing the temperature by 5 degrees each week.

The coop should be clean, have all necessary items for the teenage hens to feel comfortable. Feeder, waterers, roosts, bedding and even the nesting boxes should be ready, though they'll start laying eggs at about 5 months old. The best time to take them to the coop would be in the morning so that they get used to it the whole day unless you are introducing new hens to an existing flock. At night, they'll be confused and you need to pick them and place them on the roosts. Hens are very quick learners and you just need to do this for a single day. The next day they'll do it themselves. You need to do the same with water and the food.

Chicks are fun to watch grow. You'll notice after a few nights that they'll be sleeping in the same order on the roost. They'll also quickly establish their social pecking order.

Keep on monitoring the temperatures at night and checking how the chicks behave. If they seem to be feeling cold, you'll know this if they sleep huddled together, you'll have to get a heat lamp to the coop. You will probably need to light it for just a few hours to keep them warm. If it's in the warm months, they'll just be fine.

Chicks eat a lot of food, especially after the first month. You should have appropriate feeders capable of holding enough food for them. At this age, the chicks can be given treats, worms, insects, food scrapings .they may even look for these themselves. It also reduces their reliance on commercial feeds thus reducing your operating costs. Clean water should always be available.

Even when you take them to the coop, chicks need constant attention and loving. For one, you bond with them and they get used to people such that they don't run away from them. Secondly if you have other pets in the home, dogs and cats for instance, you introduce them to each other early on. With this, there will be no aggression or deadly outcomes. When you take time to observe your chicks, it's likely you'll notice any slight change in behavior which normally signifies illness. You'll be able to isolate the chick and treat it early on.

Chapter 5: Keeping the Chicken Coop and Run Clean

Probably this is the only part of raising chicken that most people dread. Cleaning the coop and the run, however, if you have decided to raise chicken and enjoy having a daily supply of fresh eggs, you simply have no choice but to take care of them. Cleaning the coop keeps the chicken healthy and happy. Happy chicken are very productive, so it's a win-win situation. The chicken coop, being located within your homestead, might bring some bad odors to your house or worse still, to your neighbor's house. The last thing you want is a neighbor complaining about your chickens. However, with a few tricks we will be looking at in this chapter, you will easily handle this with minimum effort.

CC0 Public Domain pixabuy.com

First thing, let's try to understand our hens. Hens don't pass urine; they just poop some stuff that is more liquid than solid. They do so several times a day. This poop contains ammonia fumes which gives it the bad smell when it eventually breaks down. Chicken will poop a lot while they sleep and since they sleep in the same spot each night, they will be huge collection of this poop at this place if you don't intervene.

Having said that, you need to ensure you have a dropping board. This should be placed below the roosts. It makes cleaning easier since you just have to take up the board and clean it then return it. This means that the board should be light and made of an easy to clean surface. Have a strong wired brush to the cleaning. You can choose to the cleaning daily or after a few days. This will largely depend on the number of hens you have. If there are 5 or less, there's no need to do it daily. If there are more than 5, then you need to clean this board daily. A plastic dropping board is the easiest to clean. Some commercial coops will have these dropping boards installed in them. If you have built your own coop, or the one you bought doesn't have one, you can easily improvise. The droppings you collect will be a good source of manure for your garden, but you need to let them decompose first. Still on this, it will help if your roosts are removable since at times, the hens will drop their stuff on the roosts and you need to clean them. Once in a while, you'll need to disinfect your entire coop with an animal friendly disinfectant such as oxine or vinegar. The dropping board and the roosts will need extra attention to fight bacteria, viruses and fungi which can make your hens ill.

Bedding on the coop floor will minimize your cleaning needs to a great extent. The right bedding will be able to absorb the chicken poop, dry it up and aid in its breakdown. It will also absorb the smell. Bedding will also keep the hen dry and occupied when it scratches around looking for insects. Chickens are miserable on hard floors since they have that need to keep on scratching. There are various options to explore on beddings. Wood shavings are a good choice since they are easily available and cheap. They keep the coop dry due to their absorbent nature and are easy to clean up when you want to get them out. During the cold months, they provide much needed warmth. Unlike saw dust, shavings are not dusty. Hay is also a good choice. Just like wood shavings, hay is easily available and cheap. However hay can attract mites. They can keep your hens busy pecking at them but it will best not to attract them in the first place. If your hay attracts these mites, apply barn lime and change the hay weekly. If you live in a very cold place, you need to protect the hens properly. The deep litter method where you let the chosen bedding to build up over a longer period of time would be best. The decomposition of the manure and the beddings will generate warmth. You need to add barn lime to keep the odor in check. A little ash will help keep mites and lice at bay.

If you are really sensitive to any smell coming out of the coop to your house or to a neighbors' you can try these additional tips.

Avoid spilling any water in the coop and if you do make sure you clean it immediately. Moisture mixed with beddings and manure will release that unwanted smell. The moisture will create that ammonia gas from the manure. If your waterer tends to spill a lot, look out for another type. A fount style waterer is better that the open faced waterers.

Stagnant air in the coop encourages the bad odor to linger on and spread to other areas. You can install a box fan to help in the air circulation. This will be good for your hens since they need that fresh air. In areas where it's very hot, the fan will help along way. Hens easily get stressed by heat which affects their productivity. A fan will keep things cool.

CC0 Public Domain pixabay.com

Fresh herbs and flowers are another way to fight the bad odors. They introduce the fresh smell and repel flying insects too.

The bedding should be removed every two weeks and a new supply brought on. This ensures there is no accumulation of manure which can harbor the bad smells. Old beddings are also likely to harbor germs and bacteria. During the winter you can sprinkle some Diatomaceous Earth powder under the fresh bedding to absorb moisture and odors when you don't have to remove the bedding. .

Chapter 6: How to Feed Chickens

Chickens are good feeders. They will eat almost everything offered to them. As such, there is not really a right way to feed them especially backyard chickens. Commercial chickens may need detailed feeding programs due to their huge numbers and controlling costs. However, backyard chickens will get to feed on what is available. But since we want them to produce eggs for us constantly, we need to make sure we are feeding them something close to what they need. Just like any other animals, chickens will need a balanced diet and will also get fat when fed excessively. The thing with knowing whether you are feeding your chickens right will be mostly through observation and trial and error. Other variables such as the weather, stage of growth, activity levels, and type of breed will influence feeding. So the information that I will provide here should only act as a guideline. The important thing is to understand your particular hens and behavior in order to note any changes that may require a feeding intervention.

The first thing to note is that the more area your chickens have, the less they'll rely on food from you. This is because they are able to forage and look for insects, small animals, worms and plant shoots to feed on. As a matter of fact they love these more than anything else. These are nutritious for them and cannot cause any health problem. If your chickens are free rangers, you'll just need a little commercial feed for them to keep them well fed. On the other hand, chickens that never leave the coop and fully depend on being feed need large quantities of food. If you fail to provide it, they might turn on each other or the wooden surfaces of the coop. Hungry hens are really angry hens. You'll also spend too much money which will beat your purpose of raising hens for eggs.

CC0 Public Domain pixabay.com

How to feed chicks

Chicks will normally depend on commercial feeds. This is because they are too young to forage themselves and they also need this early boost to develop properly. The feeds will normally be called starter feeds. You can however feed them kitchen scraps at any stage. Make sure you buy the right feed ex: starter feed for layers. However, if your chicks are broilers, or you are raising them for meat, buy their specific formulated feeds.

Feeding pullets

Pullets are teenage chickens between the ages of two months to five months. The main aim here is to get them strong and ready for their egg laying life. They thus need to develop well and have strong bones. Grower rations will make sure they do so and achieve normal body weight before they start laying eggs. At this age, they will be really active and will look for anything to eat. If you allow them to forage, you'll need to limit their feeds. However provide plenty of water.

CC0 Public Domain pixabay.com

Laying hens

Laying hens are adult hens and their nutritional requirements drastically change. The eggs have a large component of calcium. This will be the most needed component in the feeds. They have calcium reserves in the body but can easily get depleted. When this happens, the hen lays soft shelled eggs. If the depletion continues, they stop laying completely. They are also likely to break their eggs and feed on the egg shell in search of calcium. A balanced layer feed should be provided daily. You should also allow the hen to forage and look for insects and animals which are a vital source of protein. A calcium supplement would be good for them. Oyster shells provide high amounts of calcium and can be fed occasionally. The eggs shells are also very high in calcium. You can feed them right back to the hen after you have eaten the contents inside. However, you need to crush these shells so that they are not recognizable. If your hen lays daily, do not limit the food as this is what she uses to make the eggs.

You should have a proper feeder that suits the amount of hens you have. This will limit any wastage which adds up the costs. Making your own feeder with 5 liter buckets or pop bottles can help save money as store bought feeders can be quite expensive. A hens' instinct is to eat from the ground, which can cause their waste to get in the feed. Hanging the feeder can help prevent this and reduce waste since they will not be able to scratch out the feed. Some feeders will allow you to stock up food that will last several days. This is important of you are out of the home for several days and nobody is available to feed the chickens. Most chickens will just eat enough food, they have a good sense of self-regulation with only the exception of a few breeds and broilers. This is especially true with adult laying hens, you need not worry that you are overfeeding them.

Feeding treats

Chickens like kitchen scraps. You'll notice that they'll follow you if they think you have something for them from the kitchen. Most of the foods we consume will be just fine for them. However, moldy food might cause illness since it already has bacteria. Salty foods and sugary foods are also not good for your hens. Most of the kitchen scraps will be high energy foods that have lots of calories. It's good to feed these after you have served the commercial feeds. This will ensure that the hen doesn't overeat on them. All types of vegetable are good for your chickens. They'll love them. You can hang them somewhere in the coop and let them peck at them whenever they fell like it.

Poultry feeds should be the main diet for your hens. Scraps and treats should serve as supplements to ensure that they are having a balanced diet. If you have a large number of hens, you'll need to monitor them at feeding time to ensure that they are all eating. Hens are very social animals with clear social orders within a group. Dominant hens might exclude those lower in the order from feeding. If you notice this, you might need to provide more than one feeding point.

Always have clean drinking water available all the time. Find a good waterer that doesn't spill around the coop to reduce your cleaning work. A waterer that holds a large amount of water in a canister and only drips a little to the saucer will serve you well in case you are not at home. Clean the waterer weekly as it can house germs. Beddings, scraps, dropping will also get in the saucer and need to be removed. There are also many ways people make their own waterers with buckets, piping and pumps, this helps save on cost.

Chapter 7: When to Expect Eggs

Hens will start laying eggs at around 5 months old, sometimes it will take longer if they hit laying age in the colder months. By this time you should have prepared the nesting boxes where they'll soon be laying their eggs almost on a daily basis. They'll start off with around 4 eggs per week before quickly getting to their peak. Between this age and 2 years, good layers are able to average 5-6 eggs per week. However, in the colder winter months some breeds will slow down production to just 2- 3 eggs per week. It would be a good idea to include a good winter layer breed in your flock to be sure of steady supply of eggs all the time. Most breeds will have close to optimum production during summer and spring. The shorter days and light periods during winter greatly affects the hens' internal body system. Remember we had said two hens per family member for a constant supply of eggs. This will be vital in the colder months. In the summer months, the supply can be faster than the rate you consume the eggs, but you can always give a neighbor or a friends few eggs.

CC0 Public Domain pixabay.com

After two years of laying eggs almost daily, the production will go down. It's good practice to replace such a hen with another younger pullet. This cuts down on costs and also ensures that you still get your eggs. You could also decide to eat some of the chickens. However, some people find it hard to eat their hen as they view it as a pet. You can give it out or sell it, but remember eventually it will still have to go through this fate; furthermore they are bred for eggs and meat. We shall be looking at how to introduce a new hen to an existing flock later when you eat one. In your flock, you should have hens of different ages to avoid a complete overhaul at one time and to shore up your egg supply.

After laying eggs for a number of weeks, hens might get broody. This is the time when it wants to sits on the eggs to hatch chicks. It's their natural instinct to do so. However, I am sure you do not want this as the eggs are not fertilized by a cock. Nonetheless, the hen doesn't realize this. They will stubbornly sit on eggs hoping they'll hatch. The eggs will just go bad and can never hatch. At this time the hen will stop most of her processes. She won't lay eggs and won't feed as normal. She'll even pick some feathers from her body to line up the nest. To discourage brooding, you'll need to pick up the eggs frequently from the nest. Rarely will a hen brood when there are no eggs. If she happens to find one egg and sit on it, wake her up and distract her. Take her out of the coop and let her range. She might try to get back but don't allow her. However, be careful a broody hen easily pecks on you and can cause some pain. Another way to discourage her would be to place ice cubes on the nest. She won't like this experience and serves as a good way to get her out of the nest.

Chicken will undergo what is called molting once every year. This is when they shed some feathers and regrow others. This normally happens during the hot summer months. At first, you would be scared and think they are ill. They are not and this is normal. In fact when they grow new feathers, they look more beautiful and healthier than before. When they are molting, they won't lay eggs. It's a time when they are recharging. This is an important part of their development. In a flock different chickens will molt at different periods but largely in the same season.

Chickens will also pick at one another periodically. This result in bare skin and can make them look ugly. Some farmers result in debeaking their hens after this happens, however, this isn't the solution and can lead to feeding problems. When you find your hens picking on each other, something is stressing them out, investigate to determine what this is. Debeaking won't solve anything. Insufficient space, high temperature, little food, lack of water, lice and parasites are just some of the reasons why chickens might pick on each other.

Talking of parasites, you need to deworm your chickens regularly. Backyard chickens are affected by worms due to the limited space in which they operate. The worms build up in the digestive tracts, hatch eggs which are passed out in the dropping infecting other hens and ensuring the life cycle continues. The worms impair the health of your hens and affects production. You need to deworm them regularly and practice good poultry husbandry to fight against these worms.

In severe cases of infestation, the worms are likely to find their way into the eggs. You need to purchase approved wormers for your chicken if you suspect they have worms. One way to notice is through the dropping. You may find tape like worms or your hen coughing up the worms to the ground. In such a scenario you need to take immediate intervention. A vet prescription will enable you purchase the needed medication.

However, if you continually use natural remedies to fight worms, you won't need this. Apple cider vinegar, Aloe Vera and carrot juice are some widely used natural dewormers. They actually act as a preventative cure since they make the digest tract of the hen uninhabitable to the worms. With apple cider vinegar, you mix one tablespoon with 4 liters of drinking water regularly. With Aloe Vera, you could crush a leaf and mix it with the drinking water regularly. People often use Diatomaceous earth as well, it can be put in the food as well as in your coop and bedding to prevent worms, parasites and other insects.

Introducing new birds to the flock

Once in a while, you'll need to add some hens to your existing flock. This will be either replacing some old hens or just increasing the numbers. Hens being highly social have established order in a flock and any new addition is met with aggressive resistance. At times, the new hen can be bullied to death. You thus need to ease the transition by using a few tricks. However, despite the trick you use, the hen will still need to fight her way into the social order, thus you should make sure they are old enough to defend themselves or take a few pecks.

Before introducing any new hen to your flock, you need to quarantine her for a few days. No matter where you got her from, always do this to ensure they aren't suffering from any illnesses that she could affect your existing flock with. Chicken diseases are highly communicable and at times deadly.

After she has been alone for a few days and you have observed her to be okay, it's time to do the introductions. The best way to do this is by putting the new hens in a place where the existing flock can see them but can't reach them. You could achieve this by placing them in the run area and putting some wire mesh between them. This should last for around 5 days. By now, the new and existing hens will have established a new social order. Bring them in to the coop at night and let them start the next day together. There will still be a little aggression but nothing the new ones can't handle. When picking your breed of chickens try to put chickens together that are not aggressive.

Conclusion

Chickens are great birds to be with. They are excellent pets and most importantly provide us with fresh eggs. Most people are fond of chickens and only space and ordinance limit people from keeping them. Your hens will only require a few minutes of your time each day to care for them. When you have several family members, this becomes pretty easy stuff.

You have to confirm first that your local council allows chicken and what are the steps you must follow to get a license. Most urban areas heavily regulate the keeping of animals. You might need to find out if there any guidelines such as coop size and design, minimum areas between the coop and houses and so forth. Most council don't allow rooster because they are noisy and might be a disruption to your neighbors. Most people do not want a 5AM wake up call. It would also be good to inform your neighbors of your plans to raise backyard chicken so you can address any issues they may have. Reassure them that you'll only have hens and you'll take care of the coop to avoid any smells. If you don't do so, you may find some injunctions brought against you when you have already started out your project. If you live in a farming area, have many acres or are a good distance from any neighbors you do not need to worry about that.

Chickens rarely need the vet. When they have been raised properly, they will seldom fall sick. Chicks are normally vaccinated at the hatchery against all the common diseases. Your job will be to keep them healthy by feeding them right, keeping their coops clean and protecting them from predators. Expose them to sunlight and let them run around as this is their natural instinct. If possible provide a sandy area where they can scratch around. This is their mode of bathing and protects them against pests. If one hen becomes ill with something contagious you may have to cull it. Separate a sick chicken from the flock as soon as you discover it is sick so you can determine what it is sick from and if it is contagious.

Raising chicken is an enjoyable pastime and a good learning experience. They will keep you busy and entertained with their different personalities and provide you with delicious eggs for years to come. Enjoy the journey.

Thank you again for purchasing this book! I Hope this book was of value to you. If so, please take the time to review it on Amazon. It would be greatly appreciated.

If this book was of value to you, you may also be interested in other books by Ubertec Publishing.

Consider looking up one of the following books:

All books are available on Amazon.

Notes:

41809118R00030

Made in the USA
Middletown, DE
23 March 2017